Olly's Zoo

By Mat Gardener

First Produced 1994

This edition
Produced by
Mat Gardener
©2014

Copyright

Please note also * this project has been developed over a great many years, and so copyright has likewise existed on this series, its characters and titles, for many years. Any copyright infringements or suspected plagiarism will be taken very seriously by those involved in the project. It should also be noted that the author is a member of THE SOCIETY OF AUTHORS

Disclaimer Information

It should be noted that the characters in this book are wholly fictional and have no connection to any person living or dead, of a similar name. Likewise none of the characters in this book have been inspired by people living or dead, but sourced purely from imagination.

INDEX

INDEX

Introduction

One night after a trip to a zoo park, a young boy called Olly had an amazing dream as he lay in his bed one night. In that dream he dreamt that he came to own that zoo park and so he could do anything he wanted with the animals that lived there. This is the story about that zoo and some of the animals that lived there.

Hard Times

With his older brother Peter away on holiday in the country, Oliver Jackson, or Olly as he preferred to be known, was feeling a bit lost. His sister Sarah was still around, but she was studying for her exams and so she was too busy to spend any time with him. This meant that Mr and Mrs Jackson had to try and keep Olly amused as best as they could.

Keeping Olly amused was no easy task for he was a very lively boy. Luckily, having brought up Peter and Sarah, they weren't short on ideas.

One day Mr Jackson was reading a newspaper over breakfast and he happened to see an article about the local zoo park. All of a sudden Mr Jackson looked up and asked, *"Have you seen this?"*

'Have I seen what dear?' Mrs Jackson replied quickly, realising that he was talking to her.

"The piece in the paper about the zoo," Mr Jackson then added to clarify his earlier comment.

'How could I have seen it? You've had the paper since it arrived,' Mrs Jackson answered back sharply; a bit upset that he hadn't noticed how busy she was cleaning the kitchen.

"Well, there's a bit in here about our local zoo dear," Mr Jackson answered back, being unaware that he had upset her.

'Oh,' Mrs Jackson replied, before asking, 'well what does it say?' in an angry tone.

"I don't know yet," Mr Jackson replied as he buried his head back into the paper.

"I'll tell you in a minute." He then carried on reading for a few seconds, before speaking again.

"It says that the park might have to close if visitor numbers don't

pick up soon. *The weather's been very bad this season and so people have been put off visiting the park because it is mostly out in the open. With all the animals they have to keep, this has been a disaster for the owners of the park. Apparently they are fast running out of money to buy food for their animals.*

This might mean that the park will have to close down soon, if they can't find a way to make up the money they've lost." Mr Jackson then looked up to see Mrs Jackson's reaction, having now realised that she was annoyed with him.

'What a shame,' Mrs Jackson replied, having calmed down a bit. *'Surely there must be something they could do to get more people visiting the zoo.'*

"It says they've got a few ideas," Mr Jackson replied. *"Apparently, they are planning to let people into the zoo on a half price basis for the next few weeks. They're hoping that this will make more people*

10

visit the zoo," he then added.

Seeing a cheap day out for the family, and realising just how much Olly liked animals, a wide grin appeared on Mr Jackson's face. He could see that this would be a good way to amuse Olly and give Sarah a break from her studies.

Being unaware of Mr Jackson's idea, and feeling concerned about the animals at the zoo park, Mrs Jackson asked him wisely, *'Well if the tickets are going to be half price, they won't make much money will they?'*

Mr Jackson then answered her, partially in agreement, saying, *"No, I think they've got another idea when it comes to making money. The half price tickets are only to get more people to visit the park."* Mr Jackson then started to read out loud as he continued to read the rest of the story.

"It says here that they are planning to ask visitors and local businesses, to adopt the various animals at the park. They won't have to pay very much, just a small monthly

*amount to cover the cost of feeding the
animals they like. In return, they'll
get a poster to stick on their wall and,
a certificate or something.*

*"It seems like a good idea to
me,"* Mr Jackson then remarked. *"If
the tickets are half price, now would
be a good idea to take Oliver wouldn't
it?"*

'Yes I suppose it would,' replied
Mrs Jackson.

"We'd better organise
something then," Mr Jackson replied
keenly.

Whilst they thought they were
having a private conversation, their
daughter Sarah had been in another
room and she'd been listening to every
word they'd been saying.

Second Thoughts

Sarah had a very firm view of zoo parks for she'd read about them on the internet and she was very keen to give her opinion as to what should happen to the animals.

'I don't think it's right that animals should be kept in cages. They should be free to live in their natural habitat. They don't belong in this country do they?' she questioned. *'If the people who own the park can't afford to look after them, they should be returned to the wild,'* she told her father very forcefully.

"I'm afraid it's not quite as simple as that," Mr Jackson replied, being keen to avoid an argument

developing between Sarah and her mother. Mr Jackson then explained how zoo parks play an important part in nature conservation, and their importance in protecting rare animals.

"Sadly Sarah," he replied, *"the parks serve two very important purposes. Firstly they allow us to physically meet with the animals, which helps us to form a bond with them. Secondly, but more importantly, if we didn't have zoo parks, many rare animals on the planet would be lost forever."* Mr Jackson then went on to tell her, *"Without their special breeding programmes and the protection they offer to rare species, many types of animal would cease to exist.*

If you look on the internet you will see that there are many types of creatures that only exist in captivity. This is either because man has destroyed the places where they live, or they have been hunted to extinction. In many cases zoo parks are the only way we can save these animals."

Mr Jackson then went on to explain why some animals had to be kept in zoos for their own protection. Very respectfully he told her, *"You are right that they belong in the wild, but in most cases it wouldn't be safe to set them free.*

The only way to save rare animals is to breed lots of them in captivity and then release some of them very slowly back into the wild with round the clock protection. That is what modern zoo parks do, in an attempt to build up new colonies in their original homeland. Just to be on the safe side, they keep some of the endangered animals at the zoo parks in case the freed animals don't survive their release."

They also use the animals they have, to raise money for conservation projects. This allows them to help more endangered species. When people see the animals, they become more real to them and they start to care about them more.

Watching rare animals on

television, or on your computer can be nice, but seeing them for real is often much better. Most people cannot get to Africa to see lions and elephants or into the jungle to see tigers and other animals. Wildlife parks bring them to us instead."

Whilst Sarah had not liked the idea of wild animals being kept in man-made areas and in countries that they shouldn't really be living in, she knew that her father was right in what he told her. In the end she accepted that that zoo parks do have a very important role to play in protecting rare animals.

Sarah decided that provided they are well run and they act in the best interests of their animals, rather than just use them to make money, their existence could be justified.

Luckily for everyone, Mr Jackson was able to show Sarah, through the zoo park's website, that their local zoo park did meet these rules. They had also done a lot to help and protect the world's endangered species in the past too.

Sarah was also able to read the appeal about how the zoo would have to close down if they could not find anybody to sponsor their animals. This upset her greatly when she realised just how important that zoo park was for the animals that lived there; and for conservation in general.

Seeing Sarah's change of opinion about the zoo park, Mrs Jackson then tried to warn Sarah against doing anything hasty with her pocket money allowance.

'Don't get ideas about adopting any of the animals will you?' she told Sarah sternly. *'They must cost a fortune to keep with their food and the vets bills,'* she added, to justify her caution.

"Oh Mum, surely we can adopt one animal," Sarah replied. *"Maybe a small one which wouldn't cost too much,"* she added hopefully.

'We'll see,' replied Mrs Jackson, in a non-committal way. Later that day, the Jackson family set

off, to take advantage of the half price ticket offer.

Thinking about her brother for a moment, Sarah then spoke up saying, " *Peter will be sad he missed this trip won't he mum?* "

'*Oh I expect he's having a good time where he is at the moment,*' Mrs Jackson wisely replied.

Realising Sarah's remark to be true, Mrs Jackson then started to feel a bit guilty and she added, '*If the half-price ticket offer keeps going, maybe we'll pay another visit to the zoo when Peter gets back from his holidays.*'

When the Jacksons got to the zoo it was very busy; many other people had decided to take advantage of the half-price offer too. This was good for the animals in the short-term, but it certainly didn't guarantee the zoo's future.

The Incident

Because the zoo was so busy Mr Jackson had a job to find a parking space. *"Perhaps we had better come back another day,"* he suggested as he drove round and round the car park feeling very frustrated. *"It doesn't look like they need our help as much as I thought. Let's go somewhere else,"* he then suggested.

'No Daddy; no Daddy,' Olly protested. *'I want to see the animals. I haven't seen real ones before.'*

"Well it looks awfully busy Olly.

I doubt that you will be able to get close to any of the animals because there will be too many people in the way," Mr Jackson then told him discouragingly. If the truth be told, that was one of the reasons Mr Jackson didn't want to go on such busy day. He knew only too well that if Olly was to get a good view of the animals he wanted to see, he would have to carry him on his shoulders.

Unfortunately for Mr Jackson, Sarah then spoke up saying; *'you can always put Olly on your shoulders Daddy. He will get a good view then won't he?'*

Poor Mr Jackson couldn't argue his point any further once Mrs Jackson had spoken up saying, *"we're here now. We're all dressed up and the children will be very disappointed if we go away again."*

Luckily for the Jacksons, whilst they were talking, someone got into their car and drove off, leaving a very precious parking space. *'There Daddy, there Daddy; there's a space over there,'* Tanya suddenly spoke up frantically. Mr Jackson then hurriedly drove into the space. This meant that at last they could go into the zoo.

As the Jacksons walked towards the entrance of the zoo, Olly became very excited. His excitement grew even more when they reached the payment booth just inside the gates. Poor Mr Jackson then found he had several unexpected extra expenses to meet besides the entrance fee.

Alongside the payment booth, there was a small pet food kiosk selling peanuts and other items so that you could feed some of the animals. There was also a small gift shop alongside, selling cuddly toys, postcards, pens and other souvenir items.

Whilst the family stood waiting for Mr Jackson to pay the entrance fee one of the zoo-keepers spotted them. Shortly afterwards he came up to them with a large blue and yellow macaw on his arm. He then put the macaw on a nearby perch and started talking to them. To everyone's amazement, the macaw suddenly spoke to them saying, *"hello, welcome to the zoo."* He repeated his welcome several times.

At first Olly was a little scared of the macaw. Because the macaw was so big, Olly thought it might bite him. Tanya on the other hand was most impressed by him. *'Isn't he beautiful,'* she told everyone, *'look at those fabulous colours.'* Much to Mr Jackson's dismay, the parrot then sked, *"got any food, got any food?"*

'Look Olly; he's talking to us,' Sarah remarked excitedly. Poor Mr Jackson tried to pretend that he hadn't heard the macaw's remarks, but then Sarah then asked the man holding him; *'is he hungry?'*

"Well he shouldn't be," replied the zookeeper. *"We feed him often enough; but he does like to get attention. If you wanted to; you could buy him a very small bag of mixed nuts from the kiosk; if your parents say it is o.k."*

'*Can we Daddy, can we?*' Olly and Sarah asked over and over again.

"*Please Daddy, Please,*" Olly pleaded, with a desperate look on his face.

Reluctantly Mr Jackson gave in to their requests; he then allowed them to go off and buy some food for the macaw. After a long wait in a queue to get the food, they eventually managed to get some. They were then allowed to tip some of the nuts into a tray that was attached to his perch.

In no time at all, the macaw was picking up the nuts with his beak and munching them happily, much to the children's amusement. Whilst they were feeding the macaw, a lady then appeared with another macaw; this one was bright red with multicoloured bands on its back like a rainbow, and a white face.

"*Wow, look at those bands of colour on its back; this one is even more beautiful than that one,*" Tanya remarked, being greatly impressed by the bird's colourful plumage.

23

The second macaw was then placed on another perch with a feeder tray nearby so that Olly and Sarah could feed that one as well. Whilst Olly stayed with the first one, Tanya went over to feed the second macaw. It was just as well she did for a short while later there was a nasty accident involving Olly and the first macaw.

Whilst Olly was feeding the macaw, it suddenly let out a loud shriek; it flapped its wings and then promptly made a mess all over Olly's shoes and the bottom of his trousers, so they were splattered with a smelly white goo.

'Oh, dear, I'm terribly sorry,' said the keeper. *'He has never done that before. I think someone must have fed him too much fruit.'* Mr Thompson then stepped forward to comfort Olly. Whilst initially he thought the incident was very funny, Olly suddenly realised how horrible the smell was coming from his shoes and trousers.

"He's poo'd on my shoes

Daddy," Olly told his father, with an annoyed look on his face.

'I'm sure he didn't mean to do it Olly. Perhaps he's got an upset stomach,' Mr Jackson then replied in an effort to calm Olly down.

Realising that Mr Jackson would be very cross, and Olly very upset, the keeper then apologised to Mr Jackson, directly. He was worried that the experience would reflect very badly upon the zoo and might stop the Jacksons wanting to visit the zoo in future.

'Is there somewhere Olly can get cleaned up?' Mr Jackson asked, very politely under the circumstances.

"Oh yes Sir," came the keeper's reply very quickly; *"come with me."* He then led Olly and Mr Jackson to a staff area behind the sales kiosks. The keeper then left Mr Jackson to help Olly clean his shoes and trousers as best as he could, using hot water and some paper towels.

After getting another keeper to look after the naughty macaw, the keeper then went off to find a zoo official. When his father had finished cleaning Olly up, a zoo official then came up to them and offered an official apology on behalf of the zoo.

Looking at Olly directly, the official then said. *'I'm so sorry this has happened to you. This has never happened before. By way of an apology, we'd like you to go into the gift shop over there and choose anything you like and you can have it free of charge.'*

Olly's face lit up instantly. He had seen the gift shop while he was feeding the macaw and he knew there must be some things that would be of great interest to him.

"Can I? can I Daddy?" Olly asked his father excitedly

'Well yes, if the man has kindly made you that offer, then I suggest you take him up on it before he changes his mind,' Olly's father told him wisely. In reality the zoo official wouldn't dare change his mind because he wanted the family to come

back to the zoo again sometime, but Olly didn't know that.

Eagerly Olly entered the gift shop with his father and the official. Olly then became very excited because he could see so many things which could be of use to him. *"Now Olly,"* said the official, *"remember you can have anything in here that you want and it won't cost you a penny. It's the least we can do after the incident just now."*

After much thought, Olly chose a clockwork spider. He knew he could have great fun with that at school, and with his friends and family at home. Olly was delighted, as was Mr Jackson for it was probably the most expensive thing in the shop and he didn't have to pay a penny towards it.

'Say thank you,' Mr Jackson then told Olly firmly, knowing how forgetful he would be whilst he was thinking about how much fun he could have with his new toy. Olly then looked at the zoo official and said, *"thank you; this is the best present*

ever."

Once the official had explained to the person running the shop that Olly could have the toy for nothing, Olly then left the shop with his father, happily clutching his new toy. Olly then decided maybe the incident with the macaw wasn't a bad one after all. If it hadn't been for the macaw's upset tummy, he would never have got his clockwork spider. Olly knew his father would never have bought it for him.

Knowing how careless Olly could be, Mr Jackson then told Olly. *'I will put your toy in the car so that you can have it later. If you carry it round with you, you might lose it.'* Whilst he was disappointed to be parted with his new toy, deep down, Olly knew his father was probably right.

Whilst Mr Jackson went back to the car with Olly's present, Olly went back to see the macaw and give him some more food from the bag he'd been sharing with his sister Sarah. Before very long, their small bag of nuts had all gone and Mr Jackson had returned; it was time for them to move on.

'Come on you too; we've been here for quite a while. We'd better get going now, otherwise we'll not get round to see all the animals,' Mr Jackson then told them firmly.

Lots to See

Realising just how many animals there were to see, Mr Jackson was worried they wouldn't have enough time to get round the zoo. They' didn't get to the zoo very early and they'd lost a lot of time trying to find a parking space earlier. Reluctantly they then had to leave the macaws and move on so that they could see the rest of the creatures at the zoo.

Once Olly and Sarah had said goodbye to the macaws, the Jacksons then moved on to explore the rest of the zoo. Sarah would have liked to have gone into the gift shop herself to buy a cuddly toy of some kind. Unfortunately for her, Mr Jackson could see what she was thinking and so he quickly led her and Olly on along the main path towards the rest of the zoo.

Up ahead the Jacksons could hear lots of birds chattering, whistling and screeching. As they moved along, those noises got louder and louder. After a while, they came to a series of indoor and outdoor aviaries, with lots of people gathered round looking into the various aviaries. It was from one of these aviaries that the zoo-keepers had brought the macaws which Olly and Sarah had just fed.

Much to everyone's delight, there were lots of brightly coloured birds in each aviary. There were many different types of parrot and cockatoos to see, as well, as minah birds, doves and zebra finches.

The parrots squawked and whistled very loudly. They were so loud in fact that Olly had to put his fingers in his ears so that they didn't sound so shrill. Luckily for Olly, they were quite high up on perches and so even though there was a big crowd looking at them, he was able to see them quite easily.

A bit further along the path, the Jacksons came to the areas where the animals were kept. The first animals they saw were the meerkats in the meerkat enclosure. This is where Olly ran into problems.

Because there were also many other people who wanted to watch the meerkats, being so short, Olly's view of them was soon blocked out by taller people. *"I can't see them, I can't see them,"* Olly cried out with disappointment.

Mr Jackson then knelt down. *'Alright Olly,'* Mr Jackson told him, trying to calm him down. *'Come and sit on my shoulders.'* Olly was on his shoulders in a flash; he didn't want to miss any of the action. Once he was comfortably seated on Mr Jackson's shoulders, Mr Jackson carefully stood up.

Poor Mr Jackson didn't realise what he'd let himself in for. With so many people trying to view each cage, from then on, poor Mr Jackson had no choice but to keep Olly on his shoulders as they walked around looking at the animals.

Now that Olly could see the meerkats, he found them most amusing. Not only did they scamper about running after one another, in and out of tunnels, they also stood up on two legs and looked around every so often, hoping someone would have some food for them. That was why they were the first animals in the zoo that people came to. If anyone wanted to feed them, they could run a short way back and buy some food from the kiosk where the Jacksons had bought their nuts from.

Under a zoo-keepers' careful supervision, children were allowed to feed the meerkats pieces of fruit and other goodies which they greatly enjoyed. Olly would have liked to have fed them too but unfortunately Mr Jackson told him they did not have enough time to feed anymore animals, otherwise they wouldn't have enough time to get round the zoo.

"Oh Daddy, surely we can spend a few minutes with them," Olly and Sarah pleaded.

'Not really,' he told them. *'By the time you've run back and queued to get some food, then got back here again, we will have lost a lot of time; and then you will want to stay here with them for a while. No we'd better move on. If we have time, maybe you can feed them later,'* he told them by way of consolation. *'You don't want to miss out on seeing the lions, tigers and polar bears do you?'* he told them wisely.

Reluctantly Olly and Sarah were eventually persuaded to move on to the next set of enclosures which held all manner of lemurs, apes, monkeys and gorillas. Tanya thought the bushbaby's were very cute, whilst Olly preferred the mountain gorillas and the monkeys.

When they had seen enough of the apes, the Jacksons moved on to the larger enclosures that held the zebras, gazelles and buffalo. They all thought the zebras were very cute, especially the two foals that were playing alongside their mothers. Sarah was particularly taken by them for she was very fond of ponies.

"Are you sure I cannot have a pony mum?" Sarah pleaded hoping her mum might have been persuaded by that experience.

'No dear,' Mrs Jackson told her. *'We just haven't got anywhere we could keep one.'* Deep down Sarah knew she was right and so she just had to be content to look at the zebras.

Having spent some time with the zebras, the Jackson's then moved on to see the elephants, tigers, lions and giraffes. Olly was very amused when one of the giraffes leaned down and licked him with its rough tongue. *"Yuk,"* Olly said in mock horror; he didn't mind really though. The giraffe was hoping that Olly would have some food for her, but unfortunately Olly would have to have made special arrangements in place to do so, and so unfortunately the poor giraffe was left to go hungry. The incident did give Olly's sister great amusement though. *'Your face needed washing Olly,'* she teased him with a big grin on her face. Olly didn't appreciate her comment however.

Having seen the lions, tigers, giraffes and elephants, the Jacksons then moved on to see the pandas. Unfortunately for Olly, they were having a bit of a sleep at the back of the enclosure when they got to them.

Because the pandas were out of sight at that time, Mr Jackson suggested that they should come back to their enclosure later when they'd seen all the other animals. *"You might get to see them then,"* he told Olly and Sarah hopefully. Whilst Olly and Sarah disapproved of his plan, they understood their father's reasoning.

Being unsure of Mr Jackson's plan, Olly and Sarah were determined to get a firm commitment to return and so they made their feelings clear to him, saying, 'you promise. We will come back Daddy, won't we? We must see them before we go.'

"Yes, don't worry, we will come back;" he reassured them before they moved on to see the other red pandas and brown bears in the following enclosures. Sarah was particularly struck with the red pandas. *'Aren't they cute?'* Sarah told her mum, who promptly answered saying, *"yes they are; aren't they,"* in firm agreement. Olly on the other hand, preferred the big brown bears because they looked so strong and muscular.

Lunchtime Surprise

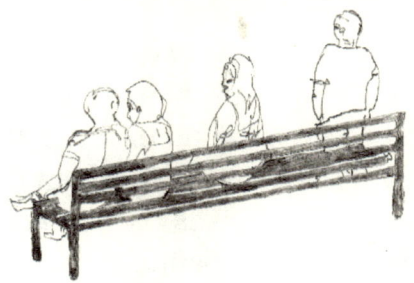

After watching the bears eating some food in their enclosure, Olly suddenly decided he was hungry. He went up to his father and said, '*Daddy, I'm hungry. When are we going to have something to eat?*'

Feeling hungry herself, Sarah then spoke up saying, *"so am I."*

'*Oh,*' said Mr Jackson in a state of confusion. He then looked at his watch and said '*my goodness, is that the time.*' He then spoke to Mrs Jackson saying, '*I didn't realise it was that late. I think we'd better find somewhere to eat. Have you seen any places to eat? I haven't. Surely they must have a snack bar here or something.*'

"There was a sign back a bit

further saying there was a cafe somewhere," Mrs Jackson replied, before adding, *"but I expect it will be very crowded."*

'Well never mind,' said Mr Jackson. *'We'd better go and see if they are still serving food. They might have stopped now as it's so late.'*

By this time Mr Jacksons' shoulders were really starting to ache and so he was very much looking for a chance to put Olly down.

Once they reached the café, Mr Jackson lowered Olly to the ground, much to his great relief. *'That's better,'* he told Olly. *'You might only be small, but you get awfully heavy after a while.'* Olly just looked up and grinned at him.

Luckily for the Jackson family, the café was still open and some food was still available. A lot of the hot food had gone, but there were still plenty of sandwiches available. With the cafe looking very crowded, Mr Jackson suggested they eat outside as there was a picnic area just round the corner. Mrs Jackson wasn't very keen at first.

"There must be somewhere for us to sit surely," she protested, not wanting to carry all their food outside. Unfortunately she then realised that Mr Jackson was right; there weren't any tables free that would seat them all. Reluctantly she then followed Mr Jackson outside. The Jackson family then headed for the picnic area carrying their drinks and sandwich packs.

When the Jackson family reached the picnic area, they were in for a great surprise, especially Olly and Sarah, for this was no ordinary picnic area. In the middle of the grassy area there was a roped off section.

As the family sat on some benches eating their food with lots of other people nearby, enjoying the mid-day sunshine, three zookeepers came along carrying some chimpanzees. The three zookeepers then went over to the roped off area. They put the chimpanzees down on the ground, opened a small gateway, and then led them hand in hand into the roped off area.

Two of the zoo-keepers then went into a small building at the back of the café, leaving the last keeper in charger of the three chimps. A short while later, the two keepers returned with some small stools and a table. The keepers then arranged the table and stools in a group.

'What are they doing Mummy? what are they doing?' Olly asked excitedly. By then Mr and Mrs Jackson had guessed what would happen but they didn't want to spoil the surprise and so Mrs Jackson didn't answer him.

Much to Olly's surprise, the three chimps then sat upon the stools and waited. Whilst they were waiting, two of the keepers went back inside to the back of the cafe and then came back with some trays full of food and drink. The keepers then put the food and drinks in front of the seated chimpanzees.

Eagerly the three chimps picked up the various grapes and other pieces of fruit and put them in their mouths just as if they were humans. They slowly drank from some beakers, holding them in just the same way that human's do. One of them suddenly burped. This made Olly and Sarah roar with laughter.

"Look mum, look Mum," Tanya cried in between fits of laughter.

A short while later, the chimps finished their food and they got up. They had been through this routine many many times before and so they knew what was coming next.

As the chimps got up, two of the keepers then removed the table and stools that they'd been using. They then, took them back over to the back of the café. This left the grassy area free again. A short while later the two keepers returned with some small rubber balls.

When the three chimps spotted the balls, they got very excited. One of the chimps then held out his palm and one of the keepers gave him a brightly coloured ball. At first he tried to eat it but then one of the other chimps looked at him and shook his head as if to say don't do that, it's not food. This made Olly and Sarah roar with laughter again.

Just as they'd done before, Olly and Sarah cried out, 'look Mum, Look Mummy, look Mummy,' as the annoyed chimp shook his head and held out his hand. The chimp that was trying to eat the ball, then very reluctantly handed the ball to the angry chimp. He then started to play with it, rolling it around on the ground.

The angry chimpanzee then started throwing it up in the air and then catching it again. Suddenly he dropped it and one of the other chimps picked it up. He played with it for a while whilst the other ones looked on jealously. Instead of throwing the ball, this other chimp kicked it as if it was a football towards one on the other chimps. He smiled greatly when he saw it coming his way. The chimp then threw it at one of the others.

Olly couldn't believe his eyes. He had no idea that chimps could play football like that. Olly then watched as the chimps fought over the ball, rolling over each other in an attempt to get it as it sped away. Soon a fight broke out between them as the ball went out of their arena. It wasn't a real fight though, they were just playing around. Sometimes one would walk up to another one and push them over, or another would be standing on all four legs, and another chimp would come along and get on its back. They would then roll over and over laughing.

The keepers then put lots of balls into the arena so that they had one each to play with. The chimps then played happily with the balls, throwing and kicking them around. Whilst the chimps were playing with the balls, the keepers had to hurriedly run and get their balls whenever they went out of their arena.

Olly and Sarah had tremendous much fun watching the chimps. Mrs Jackson really enjoyed watching them too. She was particularly fond on one because he always had such a happy expression on his face. Mr Jackson had different ideas about the chimpanzee group however. He only saw them as a distraction at that point and he told everyone, "*Now that we have finished our food, we'd better get going; otherwise we won't get to see all the animals.*"

'*Oh,*' Olly and Sarah groaned. He had a point though and so they couldn't argue with his logic.

Poor Mr Jackson had more cause to want to stay there if the truth be told, for he would now have to put Olly back on his shoulders once again.

Reluctantly they all got up and then went on their way, with Olly once again perched high up on Mr Jacksons' shoulders. The Jacksons then headed back to where the lions and tigers were.

The Final Tour

After a short walk, the Jacksons' got back to the giant pandas enclosure. Luckily for them, the keepers had just brought the pandas some fresh bamboo shoots to eat. Having realised that some fresh food had arrived; the pandas were now well awake and happily munching on some fresh green shoots.

"Aren't they cute?" Mrs Jackson told Sarah with a big sigh. '*I prefer the red ones Mum. They are far more cuddly,*' she answered back swiftly and truthfully, referring to the red pandas she had been looking at before lunch.

"I suppose you've got a point,"

Mrs Jackson conceded. Olly wasn't so interested however, for he wanted to see the bears again. Knowing that time was fast running out, Mr Jackson then persuaded Mrs Jackson to leave the pandas so that Olly could look at the bears, before they moved on to the other enclosures they hadn't seen yet. Once Olly had had a good look at the bears, the family then moved on to the next enclosure. '*Wow*,' said Olly as he spotted the polar bears. *'They are huge. They are even better than the brown bears.'*

Mr Jackson liked the look of the polar bears too, but not as much as a particular lion he had seen earlier. Once Olly had had his fill of the polar bears, they then went on to the next set of enclosures. The animals in those enclosures amused everyone.

Suddenly the Jacksons came across a whole lot of penguins. Each enclosure had a different type of penguin from another part of the world. Some were very big, whilst some were very small. Others had bright colour bands of feathers on their heads. Most of them waddled up to the wire hoping that someone had some fish for them.

When the penguins realised they weren't going to get fed, most of them waddled back to their pools and dived into the water with a great splash. Some of the enclosures had steps leading up to a long slide. The penguins would often line up at the bottom of the steps before waddling up to the top of the slide.

Once the penguins had reached the top of the slide, they would then slide down the chute at great speed, making a great splash as they hit the water. Some would slide down on their bottoms too, which made Olly and Sarah cry out with laughter. *"Did you see that? Did you see that?"* they would cry out to Mrs Jackson, who would be just as amazed by their actions.

At one point a keeper with a bucket full of very smelly fish came and stood next to the Jacksons.

48

"Phew what is that horrible smell Daddy?" Olly asked, before holding his nose. He then looked down into the bucket and he was glad that he was further away from it.

'Oh the man's going to feed the penguins I expect,' Mr Jackson replied, whilst trying to move away from the rotten fish as much as he could. The keeper then went into one of the pens and sure enough, he pulled one of the fish out of his bucket and held it above the penguins' noses.

Being keen to get the fish, the penguins waggled their flippers at great speed and tried to jump up to get at the fish. Every so often, one would get one and swallow it straight down without even gulping. The fish were soon gone unfortunately; Olly wasn't sad to be rid of that smell though.

The Jacksons' could have stayed watching the penguins all afternoon if Mr Jackson had let them but he knew they were fast running out of time.

The next enclosures that the

Jacksons came to were very different for some were insect houses and others were reptile and amphibian enclosures. Rather than being out in the open, Olly and the rest of the Jackson family had to go through a doorway into each building.

With the exception of the last building, each of the buildings had a large number of tanks and aquariums in. All of them were very hot and made the Jackson's sweat a lot. The first one had lots of brightly covered tree-frogs, and newts on one side.

Whilst Olly liked to look at the newts and tree frogs, they didn't do very much. They just sat looking at him from some specially arranged branches most of the time. Every often though, one of them would fall down onto a twig and then grab at it with his fingers to stop himself falling any further. Olly thought that was quite funny.

Olly really liked the other side of the building for that was full of aquariums which had lots of different, snakes and lizards in. Some of the lizards were very hard to spot as they were so well camouflaged. Some of them ran around their aquariums on two legs, trying to catch locusts and other flying insects. Most of the snakes just lay in the bottom of their tanks as if they were asleep. Occasionally one would poke its head against the glass and then slither off.

The next building was Olly's favourite one. It had a big sign on the door saying please do not feed the animals. It was another reptile house. This one had much larger reptiles in it and instead of lots of aquariums there were just a series of ponds. As soon as Olly got through the door he became very excited saying, "*Look Daddy; there is a crocodile over there.*" Olly then spotted another, then another.

Unfortunately the crocodiles had recently been fed and so they just lay by their pools sleeping off their lunch. Olly liked one of the crocodiles very much. This was probably because he was the biggest and he had an evil look in his eye. There were also some other pools in the building with a few smaller thanks, these had turtles and terrapins in. Olly liked to see the bigger turtles and terrapins swimming in the waters. Some of them were even climbing on tree-stumps and walking along branches hanging over the pool. Every so often there would be a loud splash as one of them fell off a branch and landed in the water. Olly couldn't work out if they jumped off deliberately, or if they weren't very good at walking on logs and just fell in the water by mistake.

Either way they soon found themselves having to swim round the pool.

The next set of enclosures were very different for they had all sorts of insects in them. Olly particularly liked some of the scorpions and spiders. Sarah was not so keen however; she preferred to look at the many different beetles and stick insects.

It took Sarah a very long time to spot some of the stick insects because they were so well camouflaged. She was amazed at the size of some of the centipedes. Olly quite liked the giant centipedes too. He wished he had some at home in his garden.

All of a Flutter

When the Jacksons got to the final
enclosure, they were completely
spellbound. They could hardly digest
the sight that greeted them. After
going through a dark sealed entrance
chamber they then found themselves
in a large Victorian greenhouse. Not
only was the area very hot, it was also
very moist, making them feel as if
they were in a tropical country. All
around them there was tropical
vegetation. There were hundreds of
brightly coloured butterflies flitting
too and fro.

      Because it was so hot and Mr
Jackson's shoulders were aching
again, he lowered Olly to the ground
and told him he'd have to walk for a
while. Olly couldn't complain, for the
butterflies were everywhere, he
couldn't fail to see them.

All of a sudden their numbers greatly increased. Large clouds of butterflies suddenly took flight, having been disturbed by the family as they brushed against the foliage of the shrubbery around them.

The butterflies were so bright in colour that they were dazzling; beautiful, metallic blues, greens, reds and yellows. Any colour you could think of was there, fluttering around before their eyes.

'This is amazing,' Mrs Jackson remarked. *'I can't get over just how beautiful they are. I've always liked butterflies, but I never dreamt I'd see some as beautiful as these.'*

"They come from all over the world. They have lots like this in other parts of the world," Mr Jackson then pointed out, trying to sound knowledgeable about them. He didn't really know much about them however; he was just pointing out what he understood from the many information boards placed around the building.

Olly had a very lucky encounter with one of the keepers while he was in the butterfly house. After spotting Olly, the keeper walked up to him and then told him to close his eyes. He then sprayed a sugary solution on the palm of Olly's hand.

The keeper then told Olly to hold out his hand out, keeping his arm perfectly still. Olly didn't know what to expect; neither did Mr and Mrs Jackson, or Sarah. They soon got a very pleasant surprise though, for a short time later, lots of different types of butterflies started landing on Olly's hand and along his arm. They had been attracted by the sugary solution the man had sprayed onto Olly's hand.

A short time later the keeper told Olly to open his eyes very slowly, but to still keep his hand and arm where it was. Olly could hardly believe his eyes when he saw all the butterflies sitting on his hand. *Wow,* he said. *'Look Mummy; look Daddy. Can you see them all?'*

"Yes I think they like you," Mr

Jackson replied, being pleased to see the great smile on Olly's face.

'Yes, they do like you don't they?' Mrs Jackson agreed, looking slightly jealous.

A short time later, the keeper sprayed some of the sugary solution onto Mrs Jackson's hand and onto Sarah's, so that they could enjoy the same experience too. Soon the whole family had big smiles on their faces as they watched the butterflies feeding on their hands.

Whilst Mrs Jackson and Sarah were enjoying their butterfly experiences, the keeper then offered to show Olly and Mr Jackson a private area which was tucked away out of sight behind a screen. In that area there were a series of cages with many different sorts of caterpillars in them.

The keeper then lifted out some of the caterpillars on his fingers and used a chart to show which of the butterflies they would turn into. Some of them were very colourful. The keeper then explained that these were the most poisonous ones. That was why they were bright colours; like the frogs Olly had seen earlier.

The keeper then explained that when creatures are brightly coloured, it is a warning to other creatures not to eat them because they are poisonous.

Some of the other caterpillars were very prickly; some had great big horns coming out of their heads and tales. Olly tried to touch some of them, "*Ouch*," he said in mock horror. Olly really liked these, for some of them looked like monsters.

Some of the other caterpillars were very hairy. Again the zookeeper explained that the hairy ones were also poisonous and so he wouldn't let Olly touch those. The keeper then explained that when a bird or creature attacks these caterpillars, they shed their hairs and they make a creature ill if they swallow them. Once a creature has tried to eat one they certainly wouldn't ever eat any more.

When Olly had seen enough of the caterpillars, the zookeeper took

Olly and Mr Jackson back to Mrs Jackson and Sarah. He then pointed out a hatching area where the family could actually watch some of the butterflies hatching.

When the Jacksons saw the butterflies emerging from their chrysalis, they could hardly believe their eyes; it was such a beautiful process. They had never thought about how butterflies come into being before, and they certainly had never seen the process under way.

Whilst the Jacksons were really enjoying their time in the butterfly house, unfortunately time was fast running out. A short time later the keeper gave them the sad news that the zoo would be closing soon.

'I can't understand where the time has gone this afternoon,' Mrs Jackson remarked sadly.

"I know; it only seems a short while ago that we were sitting eating our sandwiches watching the chimpanzees doesn't it?" Mr Jackson replied. He then looked down at his

watch and said, *"We'd better get going. We don't want to get locked in do we?"*

Olly and Sarah were very disappointed to think that their zoo visit was about to come to an end. Mrs Jackson was also very disappointed to leave the butterfly house too.

'Can we come back again soon?' Sara pleaded to her mother.

"Well I don't see why not," she replied. *"I hadn't realised there so much to see. I would certainly like to come back and see these butterflies again sometime."*

Looking directly up at his father, Olly then started pleading too.

'Can we come here again Daddy, can we?'

"Well we'll have to see," Mr Jackson replied. *"Today we only paid half price because of the special offer, but if we come again next time we will all have to pay the full amount."*

'Oh I don't mind paying full price Daddy. I will save up all my

pocket money. Please let me come here again; please.'

"Well we might be able to arrange one more visit later in the year," Mr Jackson then told Olly sympathetically, realising just how much he had enjoyed the day.

Fortunately Olly accepted his answer with good grace, much to Mr Jackson's relief.

With that issue settled, the Jackson family then left the butterfly house and headed back towards the entrance to the zoo.

Personal Favourites

It was now quite late in the afternoon and many of the other visitors to the conservation park had already left to go home. This made it much easier for both Olly and Mr Jackson.

Because there were less people around, Olly could see the animals perfectly well at ground level without him needing to be on Mr Jackson's shoulders. With his back and shoulders now aching terribly, Mr Jackson was only too keen to put Olly back down on the ground if the truth be told. *'I'm going to put you down now Olly,'* Mr Jackson told him firmly.

'There's no need for you to be up there now is there? Now that there aren't so many people in your way,' *you will be able to see all the animals*

perfectly well won't you?

Very carefully, Mr Brown then lifted Olly down from his shoulders. Initially Olly protested. "*Oh Daddy; I'm tired,*" he told Mr Jackson.

'How can you be tired Olly? Mr Jackson told him sternly, before adding, *you've been riding on my shoulders for most of the day haven't you? You have hardly walked at all today. My shoulders are aching so much now I don't think I can carry you any further. You just try walking for a while and if you still feel tired a bit further on then I'll lift you up on my shoulders again.'*

To start off with, Olly was very disappointed to think he'd have to walk. His attitude soon changed when he realised that he could now go right up to the wire in the animal cages though.

Because Olly could now go right up to the wire netting of each enclosure, he could get an even better view of the tigers and other animals than he'd had when he'd been up on his Dad's shoulders. Olly was only too happy to walk the rest of the way from then on.

As the Jackson family walked past the various enclosures on the way back towards the entrance, they had another quick look at the animals as they passed them. They then thought how thin many of the animals looked.

The Jacksons suddenly began to feel very sorry for the various animals around them, especially young Olly and Sarah. They then looked at the various posters around them, showing the animal's pictures, and giving their individual names. Olly and Sarah then started asking how much it would cost to adopt each one.

Even Mrs Jackson started to feel sorry for the various animals around them as she read just how little it cost to sponsor each one.

'Well maybe we could adopt one each,' Mrs Jackson then *suggested to the rest of the family, much to their great surprise. 'That's not going to cost us as much as I*

thought. I'll sponsor one of the chimpanzees,' she announced.

'It'll be just like having another child; but fortunately he won't be living with us,' Mrs Jackson then added, smiling at Mr Jackson and Sarah. Fully understanding her joke, they both grinned back at her, whilst partially looking at young Olly. He didn't understand the joke at all. Olly certainly didn't realise they were talking about him. He was too interested in looking at all the animals around him.

After much thought, Mrs Jackson decided to sponsor one of the chimpanzees they'd seen earlier called Billy. Not wanting to be left out, Mr Jackson agreed to sponsor a lion called Claude.

Although Sarah liked a lot of the animals, she had great difficulty choosing one, for many of the animals she had taken a liking to already had sponsors. In the end she decided to sponsor a giraffe called Minnie. She was the one that had tried to lick Olly earlier.

If the truth be told, Sarah would rather have sponsored some of the zebras, but like the penguins, they had already been sponsored and so she had to settle for the giraffe called Minnie.

"Now what animal would you like to look after?" Mr Jackson then asked Olly. *'Oh I'd like to look after a crocodile,'* he said with a cheerful smile.

Everyone thought Olly's plan to adopt a crocodile was a bit strange, but they remembered just how much he liked the look of one called Albert, and so they finally agreed to his request.

Once Mr Jackson had given the zoo their details and paid them some money, they then left the zoo. They were feeling very proud of themselves, knowing they had done something to ease the plight of those poor animals.

Eagerly, the various members of the Jackson family waited at home for their certificates to arrive. As each day went by they grew more and more impatient. When their certificates did eventually arrive, they unpacked them excitedly.

Besides getting a certificate, they each got a colour picture of their chosen animal to put on display somewhere. Olly had his crocodile picture put up on his bedroom wall. The others soon did the same with theirs.

Mr Jackson put the lion on one side of his and Mrs Jackson's bedroom and Mrs Jackson put her chimpanzee on the other side. Sarah put her poster of Minnie up at the end of her bed. She'd always wanted a horse, and this was about as close as she was likely to get. There was no way she could have a horse in the city.

The adoption of these creatures was to have a great impact upon young Olly, as it turned out. One night he had some very remarkable dreams, which featured some of the animals from the zoo park they'd visited earlier.

Albert Comes Home

As Olly lay sleeping one night, he had a series of dreams. In those dreams, he imagined that he had sponsored the entire zoo and that he owned all the animals. As far as Olly was concerned, they were his to do as he pleased. During this series of dreams, he decided to bring some of the animals home with him, as his personal pets.

First of all, Olly brought home the crocodile he had sponsored, the one called Albert, who he'd taken a particular liking to when he'd been at the zoo. It took him a long time to get Albert home however, for being a crocodile he couldn't walk very fast.

When he eventually got him home, Olly's parents were most surprised.

"We didn't expect you to bring him home dear," Mrs Jackson told him.

"Where's he going to stay?" she asked.

'Oh he can live in our pond,' Olly replied.

"I'm afraid it isn't really big enough for him dear. Crocodiles need lots of space," Mrs Jackson answered back, somewhat alarmed. *"Crocodiles need lots of exercise you know; and besides, he might eat all our fish,"* she added wisely.

'Oh,' said Olly, not being sure what to do next; then a smile came to his face as he remembered that there was a swimming baths nearby. In his dream he decided to take Albert off to the swimming baths for some exercise. Things didn't really go to plan though, for the pool attendant wouldn't let him in.

"I'm sorry we don't allow crocodiles in our swimming pool.

You'll have to take him somewhere else," the attendant told him sternly.

In the end, the matter was taken out of the pool attendant's hands though, because Albert could smell the water nearby. The crocodile became very excited and he pulled Olly forwards, towards the swimming pool. Albert moved so quickly that neither Olly, nor the pool attendant, could stop him.

A short time later there was a gentle splash as Albert slid into the pool. Suddenly there were lots of screams, as the people in the pool realised there was a crocodile swimming amongst them. Hurriedly, they ran up the steps of the pool and climbed out of the water as quickly as they could.

Albert didn't take any notice of them however. He was having too much of a good time swimming in the pool. Once the crocodile had had his swim he felt very contented and was ready for a long sleep after all his exercising. Slowly he and Olly made their way back home.

By then it was dinner time in Olly's dream and he imagined himself sitting at the table eating his dinner. Although he put a bowl full of meat on the floor in front of Albert, he didn't touch it. Oh dear, thought Olly, I hope he is not ill. Maybe he has got toothache. Just to make sure he hadn't, Olly decided to take him to see the dentist.

He phoned up the dentist's surgery and said, 'I'd like to make an appointment. I think my friend Albert has got toothache.'

"Oh dear," the dentist's receptionist on the other end of the phone replied. *"I'll see if we can fit him in this afternoon."*

Fortunately the dentist did have some spare time, though he didn't realise he was going to be seeing a crocodile.

Later that afternoon Olly turned up at dentist's surgery, together with Albert. The receptionist was a bit surprised when she realised it was the crocodile that would be having the check-up.

'Now you will be good won't you,' Olly told Albert sternly. The crocodile nodded. When it came to his turn, Olly led Albert into the dentist's room and helped the crocodile into the dentist's chair. This was a new experience for Albert he'd never been in a dentist's chair before.

When the dentist turned round he got a tremendous shock. He had never had to treat a crocodile; he was very brave though. *"Open wide,"* he told Albert; he then put his head inside the crocodile's mouth and inspected his teeth. *Well they look fine to me,* he told Albert, before adding, *"but you must be sure to clean them properly if they are to last you a lifetime."* The dentist then got a large toothbrush and showed Olly how to clean the crocodile's teeth.

'Oh thank you,' Olly told him. *'It would be horrible if Albert were to get toothache. I will brush his teeth every day; I promise.'*

"It's not just a question of brushing his teeth young man," the dentist then replied. *"You must make sure he doesn't eat too many sweets or drink too many sugary or fizzy drinks either."*

'Oh *it's all right,*' Olly assured him, '*Albert only drinks water and he doesn't like sweets.*'

"That's good," the dentist then told him approvingly. With his appointment coming to an end, Olly, shook the dentist's hand and said, '*thank you for your advice.*'

'Oh, *that's alright,*' the dentist told him. *"Please come back and see me if he has any problems, won't you."*

'*I will,*' Olly assured him happily.' He and Albert then left the surgery and went on their way.

Monkey Business

After dreaming about his adventures with his adopted crocodile called Albert, Olly's dream changed. He started to think about the other animals he had seen at the zoo.

In the next part of his dream Olly imagined himself taking his mother's chimpanzee back home with him; he imagined bringing him home for tea. When Billy the chimpanzee got to the Jackson house, he ran up to Mrs Jackson and gave her a great big hug. She picked him up and carried him round the house for a while; then they all sat down to tea.

"N*ow how do you like your tea Billy?*" Olly's mum asked him. *"Do* *you take milk and sugar Billy?"* Billy then shook his head from side to side. He didn't like sugar very much.

As she was making his tea, Olly's mum then asked Billy if he would like a biscuit? Feeling very hungry, Billy nodded his head and smiled. *"And I expect you'd like some fruit wouldn't you?"* she then added, knowing that he liked fruit.

Olly then imagined himself taking the chimpanzee to school with him, and them doing lots of drawing and writing together. Olly then remembered that his school football team had a big match the next day and he wanted them to win.

Having seen how well the chimpanzees had handled the balls earlier that day at the zoo, Olly then imagined him and Billy playing football with the rest of the children on the school playing field.

Surprising though it may seem, the chimpanzee was very good considering he was only a monkey. Sneakily he weaved his way through the players and even crawled through their legs on occasion. When he reached the goal, he looked the goalkeeper squarely in the eye, put his fingers in his ears and stuck his tongue out. The poor goalkeeper didn't know what to think. As he stood there wondering how to react, Billy kicked the ball into the back of the net as fast as he could.

'Goal,' Olly shouted at the top of his voice as loudly as he could. Unfortunately his shouting woke up Mr and Mrs Jackson and they rushed to his room to check that he was alright.

"Are you all right Oliver?" Mrs Jackson asked, not realising that he was actually asleep. Hearing their voices woke him from his dream and he was forced to reply.

'Yes Mummy I'm all right.' he replied very sleepily. Wondering why they should be asking him such a question, he then had to explain to them that he had been having a dream where he was playing football.

Knowing what a vivid imagination Olly had, Mrs Jackson replied, *"Oh I see; just so long as you are all right dear. We thought we'd better check you were o.k. I'm sorry we woke you."* Once Olly's shouting had been explained, Mr and Mrs Jackson then returned to their room leaving young Olly to drift off to sleep again. Pretty soon he was off on another dreamy adventure.

No sooner had Olly fallen asleep than he started to dream about the zoo park again. This time he started to dream about bringing some of the other animals he'd seen at the zoo, back home with him.

Useful Friends

As he continued his dreamy adventures, Olly started to think about his father's adopted lion and all the other creatures living at the zoo park. For a while, Olly considered bringing his father's adopted lion home, just as he'd done with Albert and his mother's chimpanzee earlier. Olly then quickly changed his mind however and decided it would be far too dangerous to bring a lion home in case he got hungry and ate somebody.

'What a pity, I'm sure dad would like to have seen him,' Olly told himself; realising that it was not a good idea. In the end Olly decided to bring a giant spider home with him

instead. He had a good reason for doing this as it turned out. Olly knew that spiders' webs were very strong. In this new dream he imagined the spider had made him a giant web, stretching from all four corners of his garden.

Olly then imagined himself climbing onto the web, which was like a giant trampoline. Then he bounced around, and jumped high up into the air. Whilst Olly was imagining himself jumping on the trampoline in his back garden, he imagined his elderly neighbour's lawn, all covered with dandelions.

'Oh dear; I think Mr Brown needs a bit of help,' Olly then told himself as he looked over at next door's garden.

Being a very kind boy who liked to help people, and knowing that the elderly man who lived next door was no longer able look after his lawns properly, Olly wanted to help him out. He then thought for a while as to how he could help his elderly neighbour with his problem.

After much thought, Olly suddenly came up with a brilliant idea. A short while later, Olly imagined himself taking the spider he'd borrowed back to the zoo, and collecting a giant tortoise. He then let the tortoise lose in the old man's garden to eat all the dandelions. The dandelions were gone in no time. The old man was very pleased.

"Oh thank you," Mr Brown told him gratefully. *"How can I ever repay you?"* He then had an idea and he gave Olly some money as a thank you for helping him. This pleased him greatly.

At first Olly refused his offer of money, telling him, *'You needn't have given me any money. I like helping people. It makes me feel good inside,'* but then after much thought, he realised that the money would come in very useful. After putting the money safety in his pocket, Olly then took the tortoise back to the zoo.

Head in the Clouds

As Olly walked along the pavement, he was feeling very pleased with himself. Not only had he done a good deed for a neighbour, he had also earned some pocket money as well; thanks to a little help from the tortoise trotting slowly along-side him. Olly looked down at him and said, '*Thanks for your help. I couldn't have earned that money without you,*' he told the tortoise very gratefully as they approached Olly's local zoo-park The tortoise looked back up at him and smiled as they carried on through the gates and into the zoo.
After returning the tortoise back to the

safety of its enclosure, Olly was just about to leave the zoo, when suddenly he looked up and saw his sister's giraffe looking down at him.

Realising how pleased Sarah would be to see Minnie, Olly decided to take her home with him as a special surprise for his sister. As he led the giraffe down the street, he got some very funny looks. One man got a very big shock when he went upstairs to open his bedroom window. As he looked out of his bedroom window, the giraffe stared in at him.

"Hello," the man said with a very surprised look on his face. The giraffe then replied by kissing the window; she then moved on along the street, led by young Olly Jackson. As they were walking along, they came across an old lady who was trying to clean her windows. She was very old and she had a bad shoulder; this made her task very difficult. Realising that she needed help, Olly offered to do her windows for her.

'Thank you,' she replied very

gratefully. 'I'd like to do the top windows as well but I haven't got a ladder,' she added.

"Don't worry about that," Olly told her. *"I'll do the bottom windows and my assistant will do the top. Just get me a bucket of warm water, without any soap and we'll get to work right away."*

The old lady looked at Olly very strangely, firstly because she didn't see how a giraffe could do the top window, and secondly; she didn't see how he could wash windows without any soap in his bucket. Soon all would become clear to her however.

No sooner had she put a warm bucket of water down on the pavement than they both started work. After stretching her long neck up towards the windows, the giraffe then started licking the windows using her saliva to lather up the window, instead of the soap.

As the giraffe licked the windows they became very frothy from her spit. It soon got to the point where the old lady could no longer see out of the top windows. At that point the old lady started to get very worried. She needn't have worried as it turned out though.

A short while later the giraffe lowered her head down into the bucket of warm water and sucked up enough water to rinse off the froth she'd put on the windows earlier. That was why Olly didn't want any soap in the bucket; because he knew the bubbles would get up the giraffe's nose and make her sneeze.

In no time at all, the top windows were so clean that they sparkled in the sunshine. The old lady was very pleased; Olly was very pleased too. He liked helping people because helping people made him feel good inside.

'Oh I must pay you for your services,' the old lady told him very gratefully after he'd finished. At first Olly refused to take any money from her, but then he had a change of heart because he suddenly realised that any

money he got, he could use to sponsor more animals at the zoo.

Realising he could make a lot of money for the zoo this way, Olly and the giraffe spent the rest of the morning doing the top windows for the other old folk in the street. Word soon got round.

In the end, Minnie and Olly had more jobs lined up than they had time to do. Minnie the giraffe was even given some painting jobs; painting peoples' gutters, window frames, and other high up painting tasks.

After a short while, Olly's pockets were bulging with money, so much so that he thought he'd better go home and empty his pockets before he lost any of it. He was also starting to tire of all the hard work he had to do and he decided to take a break.

After telling his customers he'd come back soon, Olly set off for home, just as he'd originally intended, taking Minnie the giraffe with him.

On his way home, Olly passed a large grassy paddock where some young girls kept a few ponies and this led to a further dreamy adventure.

'We can have some fun here can't we?' Olly told the giraffe excitedly.

Seeing some small horse jumps in the corner of the field and knowing how much his sister Sarah wanted a horse or pony she could ride, Olly then imagined himself riding the giraffe.

Oly imagined himself riding Minnie with a special saddle and harness mounted on the giraffe's neck. This meant that he was high up and so he could hold onto the giraffe's ears as he bounded along in a large grassy paddock. At one point Olly even imagined him and the giraffe going over some jumps and winning the Grand National horse race.

'Come on, come on, we can do it. Not much further,' Olly shouted to Minnie at the top of his voice.

After a while Olly tired of racing the giraffe and they both continued on their way back to Olly's home. When he got back there, there was no one home and so he had to make himself some sandwiches and a large salad for Minnie the giraffe. Olly then went up to his bedroom and emptied his pockets of all the money they'd made that morning.

After a short rest they both set off back to the street where they'd been working that morning. This is where Olly's dream took a very fortunate turn.

A Slippery Problem

After cleaning a few more windows and making some more money, Olly and the giraffe came to a large factory at the far end of the street. As they walked past it, the man who owned the factory came out of his office to speak to them.

'I wonder if you can help me,' the factory owner asked Olly very politely, before adding, *'I've got a very big problem on my hands.*

Because my drains are blocked, I've had to send all my workers home until I can fix the problem. I've spoken to lots of drain people and they say that they are all too busy to help me at the moment.

If I don't get the problem with my drains sorted very quickly, I will lose a lot of money because I won't be able to get my orders out.'

"Oh dear," Olly answered him, feeling very sorry for him.

The factory owner then went on to say, 'I've heard you are very good at doing odd jobs. Would you be able to fix my drains? I will pay you very well if you can.'

Olly looked at him and thought for a while before answering him.

"I don't normally do drains," Olly told him very honestly. *"I'm not sure I have got the right tools to help you."* The factory owner then started to get very upset.

'Oh please help me. Just name your price; you can have as much money as you want,' the factory owner told Olly in total despair. After much thought, Olly realised this was too good an opportunity to pass up.

Realising he stood to make a lot of money, Olly replied, *"Well I can see you are in trouble and so I will try and find a way to help you. Just give me a moment to think about your problem."*

Olly then had to solve a few problems of his own. Firstly he knew nothing about unblocking drains. Secondly, he also knew that he couldn't use Minnie the giraffe to unblock the drains as her neck just wasn't long enough to go along the factory pipe-work.

Luckily for everyone, Olly suddenly came up with a very bright idea. It was a bit risky, but he knew that this was his only chance to make a lot of money and he had good plans for such a large amount as it turned out. Olly then told the factory owner, *"Don't worry, I'll be back in a little while with the right equipment."* He then set off towards the zoo, taking Minnie with him.

Fortunately, being a dream, Olly could mix fact with fiction very easily and that is what he did. Olly took Minnie the giraffe back to the zoo, together with the money he'd made earlier that afternoon and told the keepers he'd like to sponsor some eels. Whilst they were very pleased that someone wanted to sponsor their eels, they were also very worried when Olly told them that he wanted to borrow them for the afternoon.

'I hope you realise how rare eels are nowadays,' one of the keepers told him. *'That is why they are here as part of a special breeding programme,'* he added, as if to underline the point.

"If anything bad was to happen to them, it would be a disaster. I doubt if we could get any more. You will look after them won't you?" the other keeper told him firmly.

'Oh yes, I promise I'll look after them,' Olly replied in an effort to stop them worrying. Having eased their fears, he then took Minnie safely back to her quarters to have a well earned rest.

Once Minnie had been returned to her enclosure, Olly then took a bag-full of the eels that he'd sponsored, back to the factory. He then did a thorough search of the factory's drainage system to work out where the drains were blocked. He couldn't do so on his own though, for the drain covers were all too heavy for him to lift on his own. Being a very small boy and not being very strong, Olly had to get Mr Kahn the factory owner to help him.

Once he and Mr Kahn had lifted up all the factory's drain covers and found the problem, Olly was then able to start work.

'I can soon sort this out for you Mr Kahn,' Olly told the factory owner confidently. The first thing he did however, was to go back over to the last drain pipe in the factory system and put some pieces of rope netting at the entrance to the drain exit. This was really important because he knew that the eels might try to escape once they'd done their job.

This first part of Olly's plan was very tricky. If the holes in the netting were too big, his plan would go horribly wrong and he'd lose the eels.

Feeling confident they couldn't

escape from the system, Olly then took his bag of eels back to the first drain he'd uncovered. Very carefully, he then popped one of the eels into the drain. Olly then went on to the next one, and the next one in turn, carefully placing an eel in each chamber, until eventually all his eels were slithering along the factory drainpipes. Olly then waited to see what would happen next!

After a while, the drains all started to bubble up and became extremely smelly. Mr Kahn the factory owner, then ran up to Olly holding his fingers over his nose, looking very alarmed. It very much looked as if Olly's plan had gone horribly wrong.

"What's gone wrong? Why is there a horrible smell throughout the whole of my factory?" Mr Kahn asked. Olly didn't answer him; he just looked on and waited. Mr Kahn started to get very annoyed and demanded an explanation for what was happening, but Olly just ignored

him as he looked on, watching the drain in front of him.

After a very long time, the drain he was watching started to change its behaviour. Instead of bubbling as it had been doing, now the water in the drain started to swirl round like a whirlwind. Olly then started to smile and he ran to the next drain cover closely followed by Mr Kahn.

As the eels moved forward along the drainage system, the drain they had left gave out a big loud burp and then fell silent.

When the eels reached the second drain, the water swirled round and round just it had done in the last one, taking the terrible smell with it, down and away through the pipe-work with the dirty water. Olly then ran on to the other drains; as he did so, they each did the same. Eventually he found himself standing beside the last drain cover in the system as it too swirled in a spiral.

As the last of the water drained away, it too made a loud popping, burping sound as it went. After a while the water had completely gone and the drain was just full of a wriggling mass of smelly eels. Despite his initial worries, Mr Kahn was now very pleased indeed with his work. *"Oh thank you,"* he cried.

"I will now be able to get my workers back to work to finish the order. If they work through the night it might just be ready for the morning," he told Olly with a big smile on his face.

Olly's job was not quite over though. He still had to get the eels out of the drain chamber and this was to prove easier said than done, as it turned out!

Whilst Olly had secretly been praising himself for how smoothly the job had gone, in actual fact, he'd overlooked one very important point. He'd been so focussed on clearing the drains that he'd not thought how he was going to get the eels out of the drain once they had done their job.

Luckily for Olly, the eels were

all very dizzy after swirling around in the drains for so long and so they made no attempt to escape. This allowed him to put a cloth behind them so that they couldn't crawl back the way they had come.

Once the eels were safely trapped, Olly then reached down into the chamber to get the eels and put them safely back in their sack.

Olly had made a big mistake in thinking he could just pick the eels out of the drain one at a time however. Unfortunately for him, they were far too slippery and he just couldn't get a grip on them. Every time he grabbed one, it wriggled free from his grasp.

'Oh dear; what do I do now?' Olly asked himself quietly under his breath, so that Mr Kahn couldn't hear him.

Realising that he now had a big problem, Olly pulled his hand out of the drain. It was then that he got a nasty shock; as did Mr Kahn the factory owner. The more Olly lifted his hand out of the drain, the more that smell, which had covered the whole factory earlier, started to re-appear.

Olly couldn't leave his hand down the drain any longer because it was starting to turn white where the water was so cold; but he didn't want to pull it out because of the smell either. He and the factory owner had quickly realised that the smelly water had seeped into his skin, and that was why his hand smelt so much.

"Put your hand back into the water," Mr Kahn told Olly in a state of panic.

'I can't, it's too cold,' Olly replied, not really knowing what to do. Being a wise man, the factory owner suddenly came up with a good idea.

Holding his fingers over his nose, Mr Kahn then told Olly, *"Here's a plastic bag. Put your smelly arm into the bag and hold it tight so that the smell can't escape. If you go down to the staff washroom and scrub your hand with some soap, maybe that will get rid of that terrible smell. Whilst you're gone I'll put the cover over the drain till you get back."*

'What about the eels?' Olly asked.

"Oh don't worry about the eels; just get rid of that horrible smell," Mr Kahn told him firmly.

Olly then set off along the corridor towards the staff washroom as quick as he could. When he reached the washroom, he then soaked his hand and lower arm in some soapy water and rinsed them off several times until the smell started to fade a little. Luckily for Olly, he found a can of air freshener in the toilet cubicle and so he then sprayed his hand and arm to hide what was left of the smell.

Being very worried about the eels, Olly was eager to get back to the drain and have another go at getting them out. He still had no idea as to how, but he was certain he didn't want to put his hand back down into that smelly water again. Luckily for him, a solution to his problem was not too far away as it turned out.

A Simple Solution

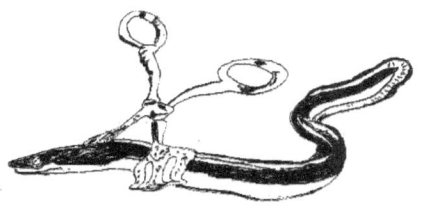

With his hands now smelling much sweeter, Olly left the washroom and started to walk along the corridor back towards the smelly drain he'd left a few minutes before.

'That's better,' Olly told himself. *'I feel much cleaner now.'*

As he made his way along the corridor, Olly noticed another smell, a much sweeter more pleasant smell, coming from the staff canteen.

'Whatever's that smell?' Olly asked himself. *'It smells really nice; just like the cakes my Nan makes.'*

Because the smell was so nice, Olly went in to investigate. When he got into the canteen, he saw several ladies working hard in the kitchen, preparing some food for the nightshift. Olly noticed one lady in particular for she was taking a series of freshly baked cakes from the oven and placing them on some serving trays to cool down. Shortly after, another lady came over to the cakes and sliced them into pieces.

A few minutes later, Mr Kahn's secretary came into the room and asked if she could have a cup of tea to take up to his office. Seeing the cakes on a nearby table, she asked if she could have one or two slices to take up to Mr Kahn as well. Surprising as though it may seem, this is where Olly was to find the answer to his problem; at that very canteen.

Having agreed to the secretary's request for some of the cake on the table, one of the cooks then went over to a drawer and took out some cake tongs. Unfortunately they were a very old pair, which had been badly burned and were very discoloured because they had been used for taking the cakes out of the oven over many years.

Seeing the condition of the tongs, Mr Kahn's secretary then spoke up, looking very annoyed. *I hope you*

*are not going to put them on Mr
Kahn's plate. He will not be pleased
if you do. It's about time you threw
those away; surely you've got a better
pair?'*

Realising Mr Kahn's secretary
was right with her warning, and not
wanting to make Mr Kahn cross, the
lady in the canteen then put the
blackened tongs to one side. She then
went and got a shiny new pair instead.
The lady then picked up some of the
pieces of cake with the shiny new
tongs and put them on a plate, together
with a silk serving cloth.

Whilst Olly liked the look of the
cake; in actual fact he was more
interested in the cake tongs that the
lady was using at that particular
moment. He could see that they might
be very useful to him.

Once Mr Kahn's secretary had
left the canteen, Olly went up and
asked one of the lady's behind the
counter if he could borrow the
blackened cake tongs that lay
discarded on a table nearby.

"Whatever do you want those shabby old cake tongs for?" she asked. Olly didn't want to tell her though. He had thought of a very good use for them, but he didn't dare tell her in case she screamed.

"Oh well, we're going to throw them out soon, so I guess it would be all right for you to have them. They're of no more use to us," the lady then answered Olly in reply to his request. He still didn't tell her why he wanted them though. After putting them safely in his pocket, Olly then asked if he could borrow a dishcloth. The lady looked at him in a very strange way, wondering just what he was up to.

'Oh it'll be all right Mr Kahn won't mind. I'm helping him at the moment,' Olly told her, realising that she was a bit worried about giving away Mr Kahn's property.

"Oh if the dishcloth is for Mr Kahn then that will be alright," the lady told Olly confidently. She then went to one of the kitchen drawers and got out the softest, best quality one she

could find and handed it to him.

Feeling very pleased with himself; Olly left the canteen with a big smile on his face. He then headed back to the eels that had been left down the drain, knowing that he now had the solution to a very big problem.

When Olly got to the drain where the eels were, he then found he had another big problem on his hands. Much to his disappointment, he found that Mr Kahn had put the drain cover back over the drain and there was no way he could lift the cover on his own. To make matters worse for Olly, there was no sign of Mr Kahn either.

Olly didn't know what to do. In the end he decided he would just have to check all the factory corridors until he found him. This was no easy task for it was a very big factory. Eventually he did manage to find Mr Kahn's office and he asked Mr Kahn's secretary where he could find him.

'I'm looking for Mr Kahn,' Olly told her very politely. She wasn't very helpful however. She'd had

instructions from Mr Kahn that he was not to be disturbed and she was determined to carry out his orders.

"Why do you need to see Mr Kahn? He is very busy at the moment," Mr Kahn's secretary told Olly very firmly, much to his dismay.

Realising that Olly was very worried about something, and in an effort to cheer him up, Mr Kahn's secretary then added, *"It would be better if you came back later; I'm sure he'll see you then."* Her plan was of no use to Olly though; he needed to get the eels out of the drain and back to the zoo as quickly as he could.

Olly's situation was made all the worse by the fact that what Mr Kahn's secretary had told him about Mr Kahn being very busy, wasn't strictly true, as Olly was soon to find out. He wasn't actually busy, busy. It was just that he was in his office having a tea-break and eating the slices of cake the secretary had taken from the canteen a short while before.

Fortunately for Olly, Mr Kahn

could hear his secretary was talking to someone, and recognizing Olly's voice, he then called out to her, asking, *'Who wants to see me?'*

"*Oh it's a young boy Mr Kahn. I have told him to come back later,*" the secretary answered him back very quickly.

'No, no, don't send him away, ask him to come through,' Mr Kahn then told her. *'Then go and get him a drink of some kind; and a slice of cake too if you wouldn't mind,'* he added, much to her surprise. Olly then went through and sat with Mr Kahn whilst he had his afternoon tea.

'I really can't thank you enough,' he told Olly. *'You have got me out of a lot of trouble. We haven't agreed a fee for your services yet have we? How much money do you want?'* Olly didn't know how much to ask for.

Fortunately Mr Kahn continued to speak before he could think up an answer and he asked Olly what he would do with any money he paid him. Olly then went on to explain how he was working to raise enough money to sponsor all the animals at the zoo.

"*If I don't, the zoo might have to close down and some of the animals living there might starve,*" Olly then told Mr Kahn very forcefully.

Olly's concern for the creatures at the zoo park impressed Mr Kahn greatly. '*Well I admire the way you have worked so hard to earn as much money as you can; and for a very good cause too. I am a great believer in zoo parks. They serve a very great purpose in society don't they?*' He then told Olly, '*If zoo parks didn't exist then many animals would completely disappear off the face of the earth.*'

Mr Kahn then went on to say, '*I remember my grandfather telling me about when he used to live overseas; and about how many of the animals he used to enjoy seeing, gradually disappeared. A lot of them were hunted and killed by poachers. They used to cut them up and sell their body parts for large sums of money.'*

Much to Olly's dismay, Mr Kahn then continued to tell him, *'My Grandfather also told me how a large number of the trees in the forests around him, were cut down and sold to the timber trade, or else the forests where these animals lived, were cleared so that villagers could grow crops on the land instead.'*

Finally and very wisely, Mr Kahn then added, *'because of these things, many animals became extinct.*

That is why zoo parks are so important. They allow us to protect rare animals and help to teach people about such animals so that they can be protected for the future.' Mr Kahn's knowledge surprised Olly greatly. He knew he was a very good businessman but he had no idea he was so fond of animals.

Mr Kahn then asked Olly how much money he thought the zoo might need.

Starting a long list, Olly then told him, *"well the monkeys will need*

107

lots of bananas, and the penguins will need lots of fish. The lions will also need lots of meat too, and that is very expensive." Being very sure of his facts, Olly then added, *"they have also got to pay for vet's bills and for overseas trips to set free new colonies of animals, and to rescue more endangered species too."*

'You will need a lot of money then Olly won't you?' Mr Kahn then replied with a big smile on his face. Olly was very surprised by his reaction. He was expecting Mr Kahn to be shocked at all the money he needed. What Olly had failed to realise however, was that being a very successful businessman, Mr Kahn was used to talking about and handling large sums of money, as Olly was soon to find out.

A short time later, Mr Kahn went to the factory safe and took out a large bag full of money and handed it to Olly. Because this was part of Olly's dream, he was able to decide how much money there was in the

108

bag.

Because it was only a dream, Olly then imagined Mr Kahn telling him, *'That should be enough to buy the whole zoo. If you need any more just come and ask me. I'd hate for any of those animals to starve or suffer in any way.'* This last comment pricked Olly's conscience and he then started to get very worried. He suddenly remembered why he'd gone looking for Mr Kahn in the fist place.

By now it was late in the afternoon and Olly knew that the zoo would be closing in an hour or so, and that they would be wanting their eels back as soon as possible. Feeling very worried about them, Olly then reminded Mr Kahn about the eels that were still trapped in the sewer pipe at the far end of the factory.

'Oh yes' replied Mr Kahn, *'I'd better help you take the drain cover off in a moment hadn't I?*

As soon as he had finished his afternoon tea-break, Mr Kahn then went with Olly, back to the last drain cover at the far end of the factory and lifted off the cover so that Olly could get the eels back to the zoo.

Very carefully, Olly took the cake tongs out of his pocket and wrapped the dishcloth he'd borrowed earlier, round the ends of them. This was so that when he caught the eels, the metal jaws wouldn't hurt them.

Fortunately for everyone, the tongs did their job perfectly and Olly was able to quickly pop them back into the sack he'd brought them in, without injuring any of them. With the eels safely back in the bag, all Olly had to do then was to get back to the zoo as quickly as her could before it closed.

'Are you going to be able to get back to the zoo in time Olly?' Mr Kahn asked him, sensing that he was very worried about the time.

"I don't know Mr Kahn," Olly replied with a very worried look on his face.

Fortunately Mr Kahn was able to help Olly with his problem, but not in a way Olly was expecting him to.

'I'll soon get you back to the zoo, don't you worry lad,' Mr Kahn told him reassuringly. With those words ringing in his ears Olly became very excited, for on the way into the factory he'd seen Mr Kahn's shiny Rolls Royce parked outside and he had never had a ride in a Rolls Royce car before.

Olly was not to get the ride he was expecting as it turned out, for Mr Kahn had other ideas about how to transport him; and for two very good reasons. Firstly he was worried that the eels might escape and ruin the car's beautiful upholstery. Secondly, whilst he very much wanted to help the zoo, despite his being a very successful businessman, he was also very shy and he didn't want people to know that he was supporting the zoo.

'You won't tell anybody about our arrangement will you Olly?' Mr Kahn insisted.

'If you do, the deal is off. I don't want anyone to know at all; do

you hear?'

"*I hear you all right Mr Kahn,*"
Olly replied obediently.

Over the years he had learned
that it is often far better to do a good
deed without people knowing about it.
There was also a third reason why Mr
Kahn wanted to make sure Olly got
back to the zoo quickly and safely too.
Knowing that Olly was carrying that
bag of money with him, he didn't want
to run the risk of him losing any of it
on the way.

Much to Olly's great
disappointment, Mr Kahn then called
his secretary into his office and asked
her to take Olly back to the zoo in her
car. Not only was it not a Rolls
Royce; Olly's driver was not very
keen to give him a lift either. '*But
what about the eels in his bag?*' she
then asked Mr Kahn. '*What do I do if
they escape?*'

"*Don't worry about the eels;*"
Mr Kahn promised her. "*Olly will
keep them in the bag; won't you
Olly?*" he then added, looking at Olly

very seriously.

'*Yes Mr Kahn, I will,*' Olly answered back very quickly, hoping to make Mr Kahn's secretary feel a bit happier. She was not convinced by their promises though, and so poor Olly was forced to undergo a very scary ride as Mr Kahn's secretary drove back to the zoo.

As Mr Kahn's secretary drove along, she had one eye fixed on the road and the other eye fixed very firmly on Olly's bag of eels. It's a wonder she didn't crash her car; she didn't though, and they did eventually get back to the zoo without any accidents. Olly was then able to return the eels back to their enclosure.

Truth is Stranger than Fiction

With the eels safely back where they belonged, Olly then went to see the man who owned the zoo.
Unfortunately when Olly got to meet him he didn't make a very good impression. It wasn't really Olly's fault however. The zoo owner was seated on a stool behind a very tall desk, and being very small, when Olly tried to speak to him the zoo owner couldn't see him.

"Who's that; who's there?" the zoo owner asked, wondering who was speaking to him.

'Hello my name is Olly and I like animals. I'd like to buy your zoo,' Olly then announced very proudly.
On hearing what Olly had just told him, the zoo owner nearly fell off his

chair.

"Is this some sort of joke?" the zoo owner asked Olly in reply.

'No sir,' Olly replied very politely.

"Run along boy and stop wasting my time," the zoo owner then told him very sternly.

'But, but,' Olly then started to reply. Unfortunately he didn't get to finish his sentence at that point for the zoo owner got up looking very annoyed and walked round to the front of his desk.

"So it's you who is speaking to me is it boy? And what have you got in that bag?" he then added, being puzzled by Olly's package. This was Olly's chance to get his message across properly.

'Oh that's the money to buy the zoo from you,' Olly then proudly announced for a second time. The zoo owner then grabbed at the bag to see what was inside it.

"And where did you get all that money from? Did you steal it from a

bank boy?" the zoo owner replied very sharply.

'No Sir,' Olly replied very confidently. 'I worked for it cleaning windows and cleaning out some drains.'

"Don't be so silly boy, you couldn't have done; people don't earn that sort of money cleaning windows and unblocking drains."

Olly then started to get very upset because the man didn't believe him. Fearing Olly was about to run off, the zoo owner then told him, "stay there; I'm going to call the police."

'Oh don't do that, please don't do that. I don't want to be in any trouble,' Olly pleaded.

As the zoo owner started to phone the police, Olly suddenly remembered Mr Kahn telling him that if he had any problems to contact him and this was certainly a problem as far as he was concerned. He knew that Mr Kahn wouldn't like all the fuss of having to explain to the police as to why he had given Olly so much money, in case his act of kindness got into the papers. Realising this, Olly suddenly spoke up very boldly.

'Before you phone the police, phone Mr Kahn at the factory; he'll tell you where I got all that money from.'

"Well Mr Kahn can explain to the police why he gave you all that money if you're telling the truth can't he?" the zoo owner then replied very angrily, being keen to let the police sort things out. Realising he was now in big trouble and fearing that Mr Kahn might pull out of the project if the police became involved, Olly then gave the zoo owner a very important warning.

'Mr Kahn doesn't want anyone to know he is buying your zoo. It's supposed to be a secret. If people get to hear about Mr Kahn giving me all the money to buy the zoo, he probably won't want me to buy it any more will he?' Olly then told him very firmly.

The zoo owner suddenly started to get very worried and he put the phone down very quickly whilst he thought what to do next. He then went back to his desk to find a phone directory so that he could ring the factory to see if Olly was telling the truth. Fortunately when he did ring the factory; Mr Kahn confirmed Olly's story and the zoo owner then accepted Olly's money as payment for the zoo.

Within a few minutes the zoo owner was grinning all over his face for he could see that at last he would be free from all the worry about how to feed all the animals and keep the zoo going. At last he could take a long holiday, somewhere hot and sunny, without having to worry about how to look after all the animals.

In no time at all he had cleared his desk and he told Olly, *"It's all yours. You are now the proud owner of this zoo. The papers of ownership won't be ready for a few days, but from now on the place is all yours."*

For Olly it was a dream come true; not only because the animals would all be safe from then on, but also because from then on, he would also have a whole host of new pets which he could play with. What Olly failed to take into account however, was just how much work he was letting himself in for.

On Safari

When Olly arrived at the zoo next morning to take charge, he couldn't believe all the things he had to do. There was a huge pile of paperwork waiting for him on his desk and people kept asking him what they should do with the animals.

'Where should I put the kangaroos that have just arrived from Australia?' one asked.

Another then told Olly they were running out of fish for the penguins and the sea lions.

Fortunately for Olly however, many of the staff at the zoo had worked there for a very long time and they were able to advise him with the many problems that arose.

When he realised how many problems he would have to deal with on a day to day basis, Olly soon came to understand why the previous zoo owner had been so keen to sell up. With all these problems to deal with, and being stuck in his office for much of the time, Olly quickly became very bored with running the zoo. He decided he ought to concentrate upon teaching others about the animals in his zoo, so that they could help to protect all the world's endangered wild animals.

Olly then imagined himself selecting different creatures and going round to various schools to show them off.

Luckily for Olly, the zoo also did a lot of very important conservation work in the wild too. This meant that he had the chance to escape from his gloomy office every so often.

Being a dream, Olly could imagine himself travelling anywhere he wanted to. In his final dream, Olly pictured himself releasing some of the creatures from the zoo, back into the wild where they belonged, and going out on hunting trips to collect more rare animals for the zoo.

Olly imagined the head keeper coming up to his desk one day and telling him that they had too many lions at the zoo, and that some of the rhinos were now big enough and old enough to be released back into the wild.

The keeper then suggested to Olly that he'd better make some arrangements to get the lions and rhinos back to Africa. Olly had never moved big animals around the world before and so he didn't really know what to do.

Being unsure of what to do, Olly phoned up an airline and told the lady on the other end of the phone that he'd like to book some space on one of their aircraft.

'*Hello,*' he said very politely. '*I'd like to take some lions, the rhinos and some staff to Africa as soon as possible.*'

"*You can't take lions and rhinos on passenger aircraft,*" she told him very sternly. "*The lions might eat all our passengers. And what if the rhinos get over-excited and start charging up and down the plane. Who knows what damage they might do,*" she then added, trying to put Olly off.

'*Oh no you needn't worry,*' Olly told her in reply. '*We'll put them in big crates and we'll give them something to make them sleepy.*'

'*They won't be any trouble, I promise,*' Olly told her in an effort to reassure her. Sadly his attempts failed and she told him firmly. "*They can't travel with us sir. It's against company policy. You'll have to ask a cargo company to carry them for you.*" She then put the phone down on him without letting him say any more. Fortunately for Olly, the head keeper had been listening to the conversation and he offered to make the arrangements for him.

Realising that Olly was finding it difficult to book their flight, the keeper kindly asked, *'shall I make the arrangements for you Olly? We have a cargo firm we usually use for getting the animals back and forth. We've been using them for years. I've dealt with them many times in the past.'*

"Oh yes please; it would be most helpful if you could. I'm not used to booking aeroplanes," Olly replied very gratefully, realising he was not experienced enough to make such arrangements.

With the arrangements made, Olly then had to wait with his bags packed, whilst the keepers and a local vet got the animals ready to go to the airport. Next day they set off very early and got onto a plane with the lions and rhino's stowed away safely in the cargo hold of the plane.

The flight to Africa proved to be

a very long one. Although Olly had planned to look out of the window and see all the countries on the way, sadly he fell asleep soon after boarding the plane. It wasn't until the plane bumped down onto the runway that he finally woke up. Suddenly there he was in Africa! This wasn't quite the end of his journey however. In actual fact he was only part way, for after clearing customs, he and the rest of the group then went on a long journey into the African bush, taking the animals with them, in a series of cattle trucks.

When they eventually reached their destination it was almost dark and the creatures of the night were just starting to get active. After a short while, hyenas started howling and lots of strange animal sounds could be heard around them. After checking that their animals were alright, Olly and the others retired to their beds. There was little they could do in the dark, and apart from Olly, they were all very tired after their long journey.

Olly was far too excited to

sleep. He couldn't wait till the morning. Despite his excitement, he did eventually drift off however.

When he was awoken next morning, Olly was very eager to get started with the releases. A native guide then took him round the site and showed him the release pens. He then explained about all the security measures they had in place to protect the rhinos from poachers. Their protection was particularly important, for whereas the lions could be set free directly, the rhinos were a totally different case altogether.

Whilst they were in a protected piece of parkland, they were still not completely safe from the many poachers who knew of their existence and possible release. That was why the site had twenty four hour protection.

When it came to setting the lions free, they had no such problems. Provided they were given their own space, well away from any other groups of lions, they would be perfectly safe. They still had to be watched for a few days however, in case they got into any difficulties finding food. In the past they had always been fed by humans, now they were on their own they had to find their own food.

Watching over the lions proved a very scary experience at one point for young Olly however. Whilst he and some of the other zoo staff were watching the newly released lions, some hungry lions from another region of the park crept up behind them, thinking they would make an easy meal.

For a moment Olly and the others were in real danger. Fortunately being a dream, Olly was able to take charge of the situation. He imagined one of the male lions they'd released, being grateful to them and coming to their rescue. He imagined a freshly released lion, chasing off the other lions and giving Olly a big friendly lick, before walking back over to the other lions they'd just released.

Realising that the dream was no longer fun, Olly decided to imagine himself on a different expedition with the zoo staff, this time collecting rare creatures to take back to the zoo. Olly suddenly pictured himself deep in the Amazon jungle of South America, with a team of native bearers, carrying all sorts of cages and traps.

Suddenly one of the native bearers would shin up a nearby tree using small coils of rope. They would then carefully place one of the traps up in the treetops with some tasty food inside it. They would then move on further into the forest repeating this process.

Every so often Olly would stop to catch a tree frog or a butterfly in a long handled net, given to him by one of his native guides.

As they moved further into the forest, a distant humming noise grew louder and louder, until eventually it became a deafening roar.

As Olly and the others walked

forward, smoke from raging fires, started to drift towards them, filling the air with burning ash. Every so often there would be a sudden crash. Soon afterwards and large groups of monkeys and other tree dwelling creatures would flee past them in a state of panic. Ahead of them, patches of blue sky would suddenly appear.

Much to Olly's horror, he soon came face to face with some timber workers as they speedily cut down the forest in front of him. It was at that point that Olly came to realise just how important zoo parks were. He could then see that zoos offered protection to the many creatures made homeless by such activity, and how they kept many of these homeless animals alive.

Olly suddenly felt very proud to be the owner of the zoo. Not only could he show people these precious creatures, so that they would come to love and care about them; he could also make people aware of just how much danger these creatures are in.

Olly knew that if people were made aware of the trouble these creatures were in, they would contact politicians so that they could talk to the leaders of these countries and get them protected.

Realising just how quickly that piece of forest would disappear, Olly decided to stay at the site for a few more days. Olly was determined to rescue as many of the animals as he could and so he made sure that all the traps they'd set earlier were thoroughly checked on a regular basis.

Olly even got his guides to set up some extra traps, even though there wouldn't be room for all the creatures in his zoo. He knew he couldn't leave them where they were and he was sure other zoos would take any spare animals that they caught. Fortunately, catching the creatures around them didn't prove that difficult a task, as Olly's guides were used to catching them.

When they wanted to catch the animals that lived high up in the treetops, the forest guides used to thread large nets through the lower branches of the trees. They then used to drive the animals out of the trees using long poles. This method was very effective when they wanted to catch monkeys and bush-babies.

'Quick, quick, there's one up there,' the guides would suddenly cry out excitedly, pointing up into the treetops above them. *'There it is.'*

"Oh I can see it," another guide would reply; then they'd run after it chasing it with their poles.

When the creatures above them were close enough, they used to gently prod them until they fell down onto the nets below and became entangled. The forest guides still had to be quick to stop the creatures injuring themselves in the netting, but overall their plans worked very well most of the time.

There were a few mishaps from time to time though, especially where young Olly was concerned. He was put in charge of all the smaller

131

creatures and this was to bring about great laughter every so often. All too often he'd trip over a tree stump or some vegetation and his jars of captured frogs or rare crickets would fall to the ground and escape.

'Ouch,' Olly would suddenly shout. *'I didn't see that there.'* He would then have to chase after the escaping creatures as quickly as he could, before they got away into the undergrowth, or up into the taller trees beyond his reach. Every time Olly had such a mishap, the rest of the team would roar with laughter. As they fell about laughing, Olly hopped and jumped through the undergrowth, trying to catch those creatures that had escaped and put them back in their jars.

'You weren't supposed to drop it Olly,' the others would tell him jokingly. *'Quick they're getting away,'* they'd then add with roars of laughter as the creatures rushed to get away. Realising that they were joking, Olly would then start laughing with them.

For Olly all that fun would soon be behind him however as this final experience in the forest was to be the end of his dreams for a while.

Back in the real world it was morning again and the sun was just starting to beam through Olly's bedroom curtains. This meant that it was time for Olly to wake from his dreamy adventures and start another day in the real world.

When Olly did wake up he was very excited, for this was to be the day that his older brother Peter was to return home after his holiday on the farm. Olly had so much to tell him about his dreams and adventures over the past week. He knew Peter had had lots of adventures too, but he was sure Peter's adventures could never match up to his.

ACKNOWLEDGEMENTS

A special thank you to all those who have helped and supported me in respect to this book. I would especially like to thank John R.S. Allen as artistic director; for working so hard to make this book possible.